W9-BXW-954

MAYA AJMERA   DOMINIQUE BROWNING

EVERY BREATH WE TAKE

A BOOK ABOUT AIR

WITH A FOREWORD BY JULIANNE MOORE

MOMS *clean air* **FORCE**
FIGHTING FOR
OUR KIDS' HEALTH

Charlesbridge

FOREWORD

If I told you that everybody in the world shares ONE invisible thing that keeps us ALL alive, would you believe me?

If I told you that THAT THING is inside of us, AND outside of us, at the SAME TIME, would you think I was crazy?

Maybe. Or maybe you would know that I was talking about air.

I think you would know that, because kids are smart. Kids are so smart that they sometimes know things before grown-ups do. Like how to take care of our planet and keep our air clean for all the people, animals, and plants to breathe.

Sometimes grown-ups have not been so smart about keeping the air clean, and we need to work harder at that. Because the air is important for all of us, but especially for you kids. You are growing and learning and getting bigger every day.

And so we need to make sure that there is plenty of clean air for all the kids, all over the world.

We NEED to do that. Because we love you so much.

Julianne Moore

Academy Award–winning actor, children's book author, and activist member of Moms Clean Air Force

Air is everywhere—inside and outside.

Every breath you take is full of air.

Every single person on earth, no matter where he comes from or what she looks like, needs clean air.

Air keeps us alive.

When a baby is born, he fills his lungs with air.

When a baby screams, she pushes air out!

You can feel air going into your lungs, too.
They are like balloons.

You can hug yourself and feel the air moving
in and out.

Every creature, big or small, needs clean air.

Elephants, grasshoppers, dogs, turtles, and monkeys all need clean air.

Grass, flowers, trees, and vegetables need clean air to live and grow.

Clean air is invisible. But you know it is there.

You can see air coming out of your mouth on a freezing cold day.

You can see air moving the leaves on trees or blowing bubbles everywhere.

You can feel the air on your skin.

It can feel warm. Or it can make you shiver.

Breezes can be so gentle that they rock you to sleep.

Storm gales can be so strong that they blow down trees.

Wind is moving air.

Butterflies, dragonflies, birds, and airplanes ride on the wind.

So do hot air balloons and dandelion puffs.

Kisses fly on the wind when you blow them
to someone you love.

Air carries sounds.

It carries lullabies at bedtime and songs sung out loud. It carries the sound of birds chirping and of thunder rumbling when it rains.

Air carries smells, too.

It carries all kinds of scents, like the sweetness of chocolate-chip cookies, the saltiness of the ocean, and the spice of pine needles.

Air looks and smells bad when it is dirty.
That's called air pollution.

Air pollution is NOT supposed to happen!

Dirty air can make us sick. Sometimes it can be hard to breathe.

In some places the air is so dirty that it is hard to see across the street.

We have rules about air pollution to keep our air clean.

And dirty air can be cleaned up.

There are many ways to keep our air clean. We can turn on the lights and heat our homes with clean energy from the sun and the wind. We can drive cars that don't pollute—and ride bikes more often. And we can always walk!

Every breath we take should be full of clean air.

Clean air is like love.
It's invisible, but it makes life better.

WHAT IS AIR?

Air is the invisible blanket of gases that surrounds the entire earth. Air is made up mainly of oxygen and nitrogen. It is essential for us to live.

You take about forty thousand breaths a day; your mom or dad or teacher takes about half as many. Smaller people, and smaller animals, breathe more often, and their hearts beat faster, too.

SOMETIMES THE AIR IS BAD

Air is not supposed to have any color or smell. But sometimes the air smells and looks bad. Smelly air can mean no one has cleaned up the dog poop on the sidewalk or the rotten vegetables in the trash can. Or it can mean that there are dangerous chemicals in the air that shouldn't be there.

Air that is bad for you can come from cars, smokestacks, and cigarettes. In some big cities you can see the bad air; the sky is hazy with what is called air pollution. Your eyes might burn, and it can be hard to see far. Your throat might become sore, and you can get a headache. Air pollution is very unhealthy.

SOMETIMES I CAN'T BREATHE

Bad air can make it hard to breathe. Dirty air gets inside our lungs when we breathe it in. Teeny-tiny bits of pollution, called particles, can sometimes even get into our blood and move all around our bodies.

Dirty air can hurt us so much that we need medicine. Some kids may need inhalers when they are playing really hard. They might have asthma, a disease that causes the airways inside the lungs to get swollen and narrow. Asthma gets worse when there is air pollution.

That's why we need to clean up our air—and keep it clean.

WHAT IS CLIMATE CHANGE, AND HOW IS IT CONNECTED TO AIR POLLUTION?

The biggest air-pollution problem we have ever created—greenhouse-gas pollution—is causing our climate to change, making our weather unpredictable and more dangerous. We've added too much carbon and methane to the atmosphere, altering the natural balance of gases that has kept our climate stable for thousands of years.

Greenhouse gas pollution comes mostly from burning the fossil fuels—coal, oil, and gas—that we use for energy. The burning of rain forests and industrial agriculture add to the problem.

WHY IS CLEAN AIR SO IMPORTANT?

Clean air helps us stay active and healthy. Running, walking, swimming, singing, and even talking can make us get out of breath—so we have to breathe even harder. It is important that every breath we take be full of clean, fresh air.

Clean air matters to everyone—and everything! Just like kids, animals can have breathing problems when the air is dirty. The leaves of plants get clogged when they are covered with air pollution. Pollution from the air washes into rivers and lakes when it rains—and dirties the water. Clean air is important to the health of the entire world.

WHAT CAN I DO TO HELP KEEP THE AIR CLEAN?

There are many ways you can help reduce air pollution. Share rides to school and sports activities whenever you can, and ask your parents not to idle—leave the engine running—when waiting in the parking lot.

Always turn off lights when you leave the room, and shut down computers, too.

Lower the thermostat by a degree or two in the winter, and raise it by a degree or two in the summer.

Recycle everything you can, to help save energy.

To my daughter, Talia, who, along with all children everywhere, deserves to breathe clean air ~ M. A.

*For the young ones in my life—JoJo & Eli, Elliot, Dash & Bodhi, Abigail, and Georgia—
in the hope that we will succeed in cleaning up our air to protect a new generation of babies ~D. B.*

We would like to thank Environmental Defense Fund, Sue and Steve Mandel, Hanne and Jeremy Grantham, Maggie and Ashok Varadhan, Adele Richardson Ray, and Emily Burns of the Bridgemill Foundation for their generous support.

A portion of the proceeds from the sale of this book will support the work of Moms Clean Air Force, a community of moms and dads united for clean air and a stable climate—to protect our children's health.

Details about the donation of royalties can be obtained by writing to Charlesbridge Publishing and Moms Clean Air Force.

Moms Clean Air Force is a program of Environmental Defense Fund, which provides funding and support.

Text copyright © 2016 by Maya Ajmera and Dominique Browning
Photographs copyright © by individual copyright holders

All rights reserved, including the right of reproduction in whole or in part in any form. Charlesbridge and colophon are registered trademarks of Charlesbridge Publishing, Inc.

Developed by Moms Clean Air Force
c/o Environmental Defense Fund
257 Park Avenue South
New York, NY 10010
www.momscleanairforce.org

Published by Charlesbridge
85 Main Street
Watertown, MA 02472
(617) 926-0329 · www.charlesbridge.com

Library of Congress Cataloging-in-Publication Data
Ajmera, Maya, author.
Every breath we take / Maya Ajmera, Dominique Browning; in partnership with Moms Clean Air Force.
    pages cm
ISBN 978-1-58089-616-0 (reinforced for library use)
ISBN 978-1-60734-859-7 (ebook)
ISBN 978-1-60734-860-3 (ebook pdf)
1. Air quality—Juvenile literature. 2. Air—Pollution—Juvenile literature. I. Browning, Dominique, author. II. Moms Clean Air Force, author. III. Title.
TD883.A5785 2015
363.739'2—dc23   2014010489

Printed in China
(hc) 10 9 8 7 6 5 4 3 2 1

Display type and text type set in Mrs Eaves by Emigre
Color separations by Colourscan Print Co Pte Ltd, Singapore
Printed by 1010 Printing International Limited in Huizhou, Guangdong, China
Production supervision by Brian G. Walker
Designed by Kate Caprari

Photo Credits
Cover: © Blend Images—Ariel Skelley/Getty Images
p. 1: © Chris Windsor/Getty Images
p. 2: © Cultura RM/Laura Doss/Getty Images
p. 3: © Jeff Kravitz/Getty Images
pp. 4–5: © Kritchanut/Shutterstock
p. 6: © Timothy Allen/Getty Images
p. 7: top, © Samuel Borges Photography/Shutterstock; bottom left, © Mike Kemp/Getty Images; bottom right, © Bartosz Hadyniak/Getty Images
p. 8: © kali9/Getty Images
p. 9: © PhotoAlto/Ale Ventura/Getty Images
p. 10: © Sean van Tonder/Shutterstock
p. 11: top, © Villiers Steyn/Shutterstock; bottom left, © Brian Lasenby/Shutterstock; bottom right, © l i g h t p o e t/Shutterstock
p. 12: © amenic181/Shutterstock
p. 13: © Ariel Skelley/Getty Images
p. 14: © Blend Images—Erik Isakson/Getty Images
p. 15: top left, © Andrey Arkusha/Shutterstock; top right, © Mike Kemp/Getty Images; bottom, © nmedia/Shutterstock
p. 16: © Aldo Murillo/Getty Images
p. 17: © Vasiliki Varvaki/Getty Images
p. 18: © Centrill Media/Shutterstock
p. 19: © Adriana Varela Photography/Getty Images
p. 20: © YK/Shutterstock
p. 21: top, © Patryk Kosmider/Shutterstock; bottom, © MANDY GODBEHEAR/Shutterstock
p. 22: © martellostudio/Shutterstock
p. 23: top, © Lenice Harms/Shutterstock; bottom left, © marchello/Shutterstock; bottom right, © Eugene Sergeev/Shutterstock
p. 24: top, © ssuaphotos/Shutterstock; bottom, © M. Shcherbyna/Shutterstock
p. 25: left, © Michal Staniewski/Shutterstock; right, © Jose Luis Pelaez/Getty Images
p. 26: © Bule Sky Studio/Shutterstock
p. 27: top, © Adrian Pope/Getty Images; bottom left, © Odua Images/Shutterstock; bottom right, © Andrei Orlov/Shutterstock
pp. 28–29: © braedostok/Shutterstock
p. 30: left, © ZaZa Studio/Shutterstock; middle, © martin33/Shutterstock; right, © bikeriderlondon/Shutterstock
p. 31: left, © NPeter/Shutterstock; middle, © Nina Buday/Shutterstock; right, © altanaka/Shutterstock